Samo Kreutz

A Time Different from Ours

ℎarsh winter
bringing spring into a room
the Kurent's[1] shadow

----

[1] Kurent (also Korant) — a fabulous or fairytale creature of Slovenian mythology, which chases away winter, brings spring and abundance to the land.

Toddler and the sun

<table>
<tr><td>

*d*eep darkness
waking up the dawn traces
a loud boy's laughter

</td><td>

*g*loboka tema
bližnje jutro naznanja
zvonek deški smeh

</td></tr>
</table>

*t*ractor noise
awakened together
me and sunshine

*f*ather's shadow
quite enough room in it
for his little son

*h*er fragrance
the whole apartment
a meadow

*f*lower under the snow
in touch with the soil
wide open blossom

*h*uge trees
from one branch to another
an airplane trail

*v*accination centre
skipping the queue
a bird

*p*leasant sunshine
traveling in a cat's hair
the sparrow shadow

*f*luttering butterfly …
all the dreams I had
as a child

*f*adybug
on the flower stem
another bud

*f*jubljanica river
flowing under the bridge
his childhood

*n*apping
with one eye open
a duck and my wishes

*c*olourful stroller
the calm rest of a baby
and the scent of grass

*c*uckoo's cry
in his thin wallet
borrowed money

washhouse
perfectly white
cloud above it

blooming cherry tree
a part of dense shadow
an old man

promenade
walking lazily
me and the road noise

Lake Bled
rendezvous with tranquillity
not so successful

castle yard
the largest crowd
around the crow

stone pedestal
instead of the statue
a small snail on it

*e*cho in the mountain
much louder than voice
my memories

*d*ecaying house
filling its wide cracks
linden tree fragrance

*h*omecoming
hugs me even tighter
the scent of a tea

late afternoon
having lunch together
me and bird sounds

granny's glasses
in her grandson's hand
nothing else but a toy

picture on the wall
too big for a frame –
a toddler and the sun

*l*ove-story…
playing with boy's heart
a kitten

*n*ight sky
so deep in the space
the child's gaze

*c*hocolate truffles
reaching for the last one
me and the moonlight

*t*he dark hours
not sleeping as I do
serenity

*s*peeding cyclist
still unreachable
a chickadee

*s*pehan kolesar
ptič nekoliko naprej
zanj neulovljiv

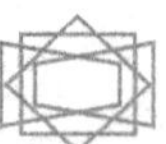

Pieces of a rainbow

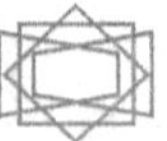

nutritious breakfast
mixed with the cereals
pieces of a rainbow

krepčilen zajtrk
s kosmiči pomešana
zrnca mavrice

first glow
in a rooster's voice
already summer

house threshold
patiently waiting to enter
today's sunshine

proud father
by a baby in a pram
glittering dawn

going to work
far ahead of me
elder tree scent

*l*ivelier than I am
fallen cherry blossom
in the wind

*s*ummer morning
marble war monument
still so cold

*g*arden centre
by the blooming flowers
a cluster of children

*s*unny season
fully blossomed
my new desires

*h*ot weather
cooling off in a pool
the bush shadow

*n*arrow street
rubbing up against me
the bell's echo

*d*isplay window
wearing a spider net
a mannequin

*b*right sun
thinking about her
youngster in love

*a*fternoon heat
I lend my shadow
to a sparrow

*o*ld rut
full of butterflies
dusty blossoms

*t*urtle dove
loud dog barking
now her voice

*s*hopping mall
coming out with me
a dark cloud

sudden shower
together penetrating the air
drops and shouts

summer downpour
under a huge umbrella
a toddler's joy

raging storm
behind the forest trees
the animals and my fear

heavy rain
like an old man
the flowering bush

lightning strike
stuffed mink's eyes
so lively

fully vaccinated
resting in my shadow
a bluebird

*s*un at last
smiling for the first time
a rainbow baby

a walk in the woods
instead of mushrooms
I pick memories

home forest
behind every tree
my youthful dreams

clear water
unusually cool
an old man's reflection

hot summer day
everything what unite us –
Adriatic Sea

shell gathering
so many memories
in my hand

high waves
riding the largest
the gull's cry

public beach
sunbathing together
me and the old boat

lazy evening
relaxing in a deck chair
the sea sound

cold lemonade
at the bottom of the glass
all my childhood wishes

drought
fully dehydrated
the farmer's hope

sunset
a girl whispers
to the shadows

firefly
at a grandad's palm
a piece of the star

night crickets
caught in their chirping
my youthful carefreeness

cat's purr
caressing her hair
the owner's words

*s*toryteller
listening to the tales
a boy and his shadow

*s*ocial distancing
avoiding me
even dreams

*a*pples in a bowl
my late-night guest
a yearning for her

no matter where I go
always first at the finish
the stars

*c*urrant bush
behind ripe fruits
spongy wooden fence

*r*ibezov grmič
za zrelimi plodovi
hudo gobast plot

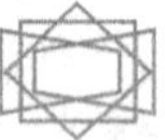

A girl's song

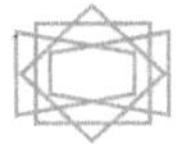

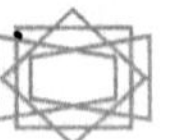

sudden gust of wind
among birds in the sky
a handkerchief

neukrotljiv piš
med ptiči sredi neba
robec s sušila

daybreak
sharing the bird's nest
a feather and a mist

staying
in the guest room
a predawn dusk

chilly morning
relaxing under the blanket
all the warmth

autumn mizzle
falling from the clouds
a melancholy

gloomy day
reaching for a cup of tea
the lightning bolt

endless conversation
chatty like always
the rain

morning downpour
spraying from the puddle
a girl's song

raging tempest
soaked to the skin
all the sounds

heavily cloudy day
switching on the sun
my hope

pale rainbow
their first words
after a quarrel

honey on bread
still tasting so sweet
this year's summer

contorted old tree
ripening in the crown
a cobweb

magpie's shadow
I wait for the big news
hatless

crows
brought by a postman
their caws

early september
flying towards south
swallows and my youth

school reopening
together with children
the shadows

*f*ast train
traveling in the same direction
all the thoughts

*b*ookshelves
shadows on them
not alphabetized

*y*oung librarian
I borrow from her
a tome and a smile

*f*oreign city
taking for a walk
my homesickness

*m*ain square
lonely among the crowd
a beggar's plea

no blood at all
just a dog shadow
run over

*a*nti-war protest
among the participants
the sunshine

*I*ndian summer
in the deepest shadow
dry leaves

*t*witcher…
observing him
an ordinary sparrow

*w*ild geese flock
out of the formation
their honking

*r*ushing river
water mill toy on it
just in my minds

*c*anoeist
rowing with him
the expectations

birth town
visiting her without an end
just the nostalgia

old homestead
full of memories
and his absence

deep in the woods
mushrooming with me
big wishes

vast forest
I once again can hear
the calmness

chanterelles in a palm
smelling so pleasant
even the fingers

hide and seek
a boy's grandad
lost among memories

long goodbye
reaching into my hands
a scent of the summer

grape harvest
bending winemaker's back
fruits and expectation

fog all day
drawings under the feet
hardly noticeable

*se*clusion…
the smell of food from next-door
his sole companion

*t*ree near the school
too heavy for just one branch
the child's thoughts

*p*andemic
spending time together
people and the fog

outside noise
completely overheard
years piling in me

an old man
faithful to him
just the past

chestnut picking
with it in prickly shells
our beliefs

a stag bellows
immediate response
the rifle shot

*A*ll saints day
flowers and memories
even more fragrant

*m*oss on gravestone
lying in the ground
the anonymous

*l*unar eclipse
much thinner as before
our self-centredness

*a*bandoned kindergarten
resting nearby in the grass
a child's scarf

*z*apuščen vrtec
pred njim v travi počiva
zguljen deški šal

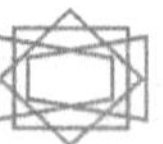

The sound of a bell

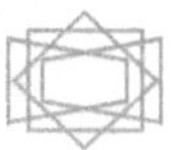

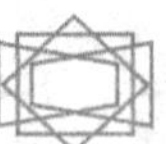

cloudburst
discarded tin can
full again

silovit naliv
odvržena konzerva
končno spet polna

december storm
without an umbrella
my vivid imagination

prolonged downpour
all the castles in the sky
washed away

musician's violin case
tossing its contribution
the rain

light showers
slightly cleaner
his swearing

*m*orning mist
strolling around
just voices

*l*eafless bush
on its thin branches
children's shouts

*s*un again
after a long wait
now in a boy's eyes

knocking
and knocking on the door
a presence of the winter

first snow
her hair shines
in a new colour

lost and found
without the owner
winter sun

*s*wirling snowflakes
a girl's happiness
all in white

*w*intry midday
gathered layer by layer
the silence

*b*athing…
all the rainbow colours
now on his hairs

*a*ttic
in my old clothes
just a draught

*g*ranny's kerchief
still perceptible
a time different from ours

*o*utdoor fitness
doing workouts together
me and powdery snow

grandfather…
using a walking stick
only his old age

cold winter
trembling in the snow
the sound of a bell

dense fog
even the words
lost

half melted snow
the reflection of a toddler
barely visible

parking garage
on the last free lot
a dead sparrow

meeting me
meeting her and him
the melancholia

*p*rogramme rerun…
thinking about the things
I shouldn't have done

tv presenter's voice
not enough room for me
even in my home

*w*ithout the scarf
wearing just a boy's song
the snowman

december afterglow
more shadows as outside
still in me

winter dusk
having a short walk
I become the night

hoping
for both of us
a foster dog

*b*lack cat
making dark brighter
her purr

*n*ight over the city　　　*s*once za hribom
New Year's decorations　　novoletno okrasje
dazzling again　　　　　　spet bolj bleščavo

A WORD OR TWO ABOUT THE AUTHOR

Samo Kreutz lives in Ljubljana, Slovenia. He began to write as an eight-year-old boy, when he wrote his first story (and later a poem). One day his parents told him that simply by writing he cannot earn enough for a decent life, so he replied that he will become a writer and a joiner. Now, at the age of forty-six, he is not yet a joiner (nor a carpenter), but the Bachelor of Economics, who besides poetry and short stories, also writes novels and haiku (since 2011). He is the author of nine books in Slovene (all published by the Ekslibris, publishing house in Ljubljana) and one in English (a haiku book titled *The Stars for Tonight*, which was published by Cyberwit.net). His work has appeared in various Slovenian literary magazines, anthologies, on national Radio, on several international websites, e- and printed journals (most recently in the *Ink Sweat & Tears: The poetry and prose webzine* and in the *Bloo Outlier Journal*).

A NOTE ABOUT THE BOOK

A Time Different from Ours consists of 155 haiku. Poems in this collection are about our time and are joined by those with a touch of nature, hope, faith, and affection, representing the contrast. They can be found (in English, Slovene or both versions) in printed journals: *Akitsu Quarterly, Seashores: Haiku Journal,* and *Taj Mahal Review,* on websites: *Akita International Haiku Network, Asahi Haikuist Network, Autumn Moon Haiku Journal, Better Than Starbucks: Poetry and Fiction Journal, Bloo Outlier Journal, Cold Moon Journal, Creatrix Haiku and Poetry Journal, Dwelling Literary, Frameless Sky: Art Video Journal, Haikuniverse: a daily haiku or micro-poem, Ink Sweat & Tears: The poetry and prose webzine, Jalmurra: Art and Poetry Journal, Kingfisher Journal, Locutio, Poetry Pea, Stardust Haiku Online Journal, The Bamboo Hut, Tsuri-Dōrō: A Small Journal of Haiku and Senryu, Under the Basho,* and *Wales Haiku Journal,* in anthologies: *Haiku zbornik: Ludbreg, Pesem si: zbornik, Samoborski haiku susreti Darko Plažanin,* and in quite a few broadcasts on the national Radio.

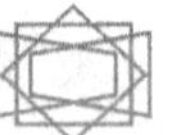

CONTENTS

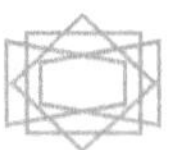

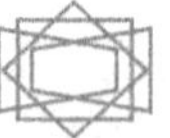

www.ingramcontent.com/pod-product-compliance
Lightning Source LLC
LaVergne TN
LVHW051504170726
843492LV00002B/795